Six-Word Lessons for

A STRESS-FREE WEDDING

100 Lessons to Plan Your Wedding Without Worry and Enjoy Your Day

Jennifer Taylor

TaylordEvents.com

Published by Pacelli Publishing
Bellevue, Washington

Six-Word Lessons for a Stress-Free Wedding

All rights reserved. No part of this book may be reproduced or transmitted in any form or by any means, electronic or mechanical including photocopying, recording or by any information storage or retrieval system, without the written permission of the publisher, except where permitted by law.

Limit of Liability: While the author and the publisher have used their best efforts in preparing this book, they make no representation or warranties with respect to accuracy or completeness of the content of this book. The advice and strategies contained herein may not be suitable for your situation. Consult with a professional when appropriate.

Copyright © 2018 by Jennifer Taylor

Published by Pacelli Publishing
9905 Lake Washington Blvd. NE, #D-103
Bellevue, Washington 98004
PacelliPublishing.com

Cover and interior designed by Pacelli Publishing
Author photo by Clane Gessel
Cover image by Amelia Soper Photography

ISBN-10: 1-933750-75-8
ISBN-13: 978-1-933750-75-0

Dedication

I would like to dedicate this book to my husband, who has been on this journey with me since we married in 2004. For all the weekends I was gone doing weddings, thank you for being so supportive.

To my parents, sister and grandparents, who have supported me in everything I have done so far.

I would like to thank my own wedding planner, Wendy, who believed that I could become a wedding planner and has been one of my biggest cheerleaders.

To my team, Alex, Madi, Brittney and Ashley, thank you for being a part of Taylor'd Events Group and loving my business as if it was your own.

To all the wedding professionals I have worked with, thank you for being there with your support, gentle nudging at times, and for being awesome.

Finally, to my clients, thank you for letting me plan your weddings. I can't believe I do this for a job!

Table of Contents

Introduction 9

Engaged!? What You Need to Do 11

What Does a Wedding Planner Do? 23

Venues: All You Need to Know 35

Finding Wedding Professionals Best for You 47

Design Tips to Rock Your Space 59

Ceremony: More than just "I Do" 71

Wedding Party: What Do They Do? 83

Making the Most of Wedding Week 95

Let it Go: Wedding Day Bliss 107

How to Beat the Wedding Blues 119

Introduction

Hi! I'm Jen Taylor, owner and planner of Taylor'd Events Group. I have been planning weddings since 2004, and yes, I helped plan my own, with help from a professional planner. I hope this book brings you some real-life advice on how to plan your wedding, things you may not see on a blog or wedding planning site. My goal is that your wedding planning will be as stress-free as possible, by using these tips that I use in planning weddings for my couples.

Congratulations and Best Wishes!

Jen Taylor

Engaged!? What You Need to Do

1

Put a ring on it! Done

Spend time with your fiancé. Do not jump into planning the instant you have the ring on your finger. Take a month and just be engaged, getting used to the fact that you are getting married. Take time to dream, to buy every wedding magazine, join every Facebook group, etc. Everything else can wait. Just enjoy the new journey of being engaged!

The talk: them, them and us

After a month or so you can start pulling in the family and begin the sometimes-difficult topic of who is paying for what. For most people, the days of Emily Post's etiquette rules regarding who pays for what are gone. Sometimes the couple pays for it all, sometimes it is the parents of the bride, but with gender equality, this has gone out the window. Sit down with the family and talk money.

3

Now singing the wedding budget blues

Now that the money conversation is done, create a budget. A good rule of thumb is that the venue/catering is roughly forty to fifty percent of your budget. The rest is up to you. What are the top three categories that are important to the two of you? Is it floral and décor, is it the band, or something else? Use the budgeting tool from *WeddingWire.com* to help break it down.

Laying out the boundaries and expectations

When setting boundaries and expectations with your family, the money talk will always bring out the family dynamics on the topic. Because they are "gifting" you the money, they may feel they can control how it is spent and who to spend it on. This is a good time for the two of you to set the boundaries and expectations with your families about the planning and the wedding itself.

It is your wedding: do it!

You will need to set more boundaries as you get advice, and decide how to take it. Will you let it influence you or not? If you are one who has trouble making decisions, this will be the hardest part of planning. Stick to your guns. This is your wedding. If you want pie and the family wants cake, don't worry about it and have the pie!

6

Make the planning fun and easy.

May I suggest the following tools to help with planning? These are tools I have suggested to couples I have worked with to help them navigate the craziness of planning. There is a ton of information out there, take what you need and leave the rest. If weddings aren't your thing, don't worry, most are in the same boat. In the next few lessons I will give you four of my best tools.

7

Use an all-inclusive planning site.

AislePlanner.com is a tool that our team uses with our clients. It has everything you need to plan and organize your wedding, from checklists to budgeting to creating a timeline. You can enter all of your guests and start assigning seats at tables as you get the RSVPs. You can invite your family and wedding party to use the tool if you like, to involve them in the planning process.

Help for where to find vendors

WeddingWire.com is a great place to find reviews by other couples and wedding professionals, along with great wedding inspirations, forums to connect with other couples and registries. I suggest researching five vendors at a time. Reach out to them by email or phone, then narrow down to three. Meet with those three, then choose one. Keep doing this until you find all your vendors.

Wedding shows to taste-test cakes

Wedding shows are great tools for meeting a lot of wedding professionals in one place, but there are many different shows. While large wedding conventions have a lot of professionals in one place, you can't really connect with them. Boutique shows are more intimate and you get to connect with the professionals more. But one thing they all have is cake tasting!

Take some time off from planning.

Don't spend every weekend planning your wedding. Take time out to have a date night, or get a couples massage. One of the best things I did during my wedding planning was to have a facial once a month. It took my mind off of planning and my skin never looked better. Take time to meet up with friends and not talk about the wedding--keep involved in their lives.

What Does a Wedding Planner Do?

11

Job of a wedding planner/coordinator

Our job is to help you navigate the process of planning, from creating checklists and timelines to finding the wedding professionals and vendors that fit your budget and personality. We are project managers, and we make sure things get done and go as smoothly as possible on the wedding day. We will be your advocate, but should not try to take over your wedding.

More on what a planner does

We work on planning and logistics, such as negotiation, budget tracking and timelines. We are there to think of all the little things and tie up all loose ends. We are an unbiased opinion to educate you on all of the options and give you advice on the best fit for you. We learn everything in advance so on the wedding day we don't bother you with the basics.

How is a wedding designer different?

A professional wedding designer spends hours finding inspiration, dreaming up new designs, and practicing their secrets to make sure your "impossible" vision can happen. They work with you to identify your vision and bring it to life. Their world revolves around colors, lighting, floral, and magic tools to make things seemingly float in the air. A designer takes ideas and turns them into a polished experience from beginning to end.

14

Why should these jobs be separate?

Both planning services and design services are in-depth, labor intensive, and time-consuming. Offering both as the same service is an injustice to the client. It will cause things to be left out in both areas throughout the planning process, but the wedding day will be affected the most. If the same person is the designer and planner, no matter how many members they have on their team, things will fall through the cracks.

Why build relationships with wedding professionals?

Vendors recommended by your planner are at the top of their field. Why do I say this with so much confidence? We have spent hours developing relationships with these vendors. When we make a recommendation, we are trusting a piece of our client's most important day with them. We know they will do their job, go over the top, and work as a team member.

16

What's going on in the market?

A planner should spend the off-season visiting newer hotels and venues in the area to see them and meet the sales managers. They should reach out and have lunch or coffee with other wedding pros to get to know them personally and learn how they can collaborate together. A planner should belong to networking organizations that can help them grow and strengthen their ties within their community.

Why is being your advocate important?

A planner should be your advocate during the planning process, taking your vision and making it happen with the right venue and wedding professionals. There are times, however, when this might not be possible, so it is the planner's job to work with the professional to try to make it happen, or give you options if the vision needs to be tweaked.

18

Project management means checklists and timelines.

Project management is what a planner does to focus on getting the project (your wedding) done with ease, on time and with no hiccups. Checklists for the client are imperative to help this along. Timelines for the day of are only guidelines. A planner's goal is to get you down the aisle at the time of the invitation.

Day of: where the magic happens

A good wedding planner knows that great preparation leads to flawless execution. Yes, there may be things that go a little sideways, but the prep will lessen the blow and you might not even know something went wrong. From the moment we walk in the door to the moment you leave, we are making sure the day runs smoothly and that you and your guests can enjoy the day and evening.

Who to call in an emergency

Where your planner really shines is in having the contacts to provide a tent in case of rain, generators in case of a power outage, etc. We should know how to put back together a boutonniere or bouquet and salvage a cake if needed. A planner also carries an extensive emergency kit with everything that might be needed, from phone chargers to smelling salts and everything in between.

Venues: All You Need to Know

Sales: the first point of contact

The venue sales manager is responsible for contract negotiations related to the venue and informing you of venue rules and regulations. They are there to make the sale, so if you ask whether they have a coordinator, they may say "yes," because in fact they do, but that person is not necessarily what you think of as a coordinator. The venue coordinator is there to answer questions about the rules, regulations, layout, power and capacity.

22

What does a venue coordinator do?

On the wedding day, a day-of venue coordinator will take over. Their job is to ensure that everything related to the venue and their staff runs smoothly and follows the requests outlined in their banquet event order. They will make sure all the dietary restrictions and menu substitutions are correct, but at the end of the day they are responsible for protecting the venue, not calling your vendors or other tasks unrelated to the venue.

What is a banquet event order?

For a venue that has in-house catering, this is the form that is critical. It shows date and timing of the event, rooms reserved, menu, bar, and anything special that has been added for your wedding. When you get a new version of this, review it thoroughly. This is the document that the venue and kitchen will use on your wedding day.

Working with an off-site caterer

Some venues are just that--a space. They do not have an exclusive caterer or in-house kitchen staff. When you use a venue that allows you to bring in an outside caterer, make sure the caterer is reputable and has done weddings, can supply bartenders, has insurance for liability and can work with dietary restrictions.

25

How many hours do you have?

You need to understand this going in. How many hours do you have in the venue, and when do the hours start counting? Is it when the first vendor arrives, or is there a designated time slot? Knowing this will make creating a timeline much easier and help you communicate when your vendors can arrive for setup, décor, etc. You also need to know when everyone must be OUT of the venue.

What's included in the facility fee?

This fee can be anything. It can be only the cost of using the venue and the coordinator. It could also include tables, chairs, audio/video, set up of the tables and chairs and takedown. Some venues have different options for how many hours you can use the venue and other perks. Ask what the fee includes if you do not see this information in the packet they provide to you.

On the day of the wedding

You arrive at the venue; the coordinator is there making sure you are all settled in. They then go off and start their day, which could be giving tours to potential clients or finishing the last bit of communication to their staff about your wedding. At some point during the day they pass you off to their lead person, to make sure the rest of the event runs smoothly.

Why is there a service charge?

The service charge is a mandatory and automatic fee that is added to your catering or venue contract. This charge and any other fees are almost always listed in the fine print at the bottom of the documents with your initial price brochures. Most caterers, venues and hotels charge a twenty to twenty-two percent service charge. This is applied to the entire bill--food, beverage, staffing, and any upgrade charges.

What the *&%$ does it cover?

The exact breakdown of what this service charge covers is different for each caterer/venue. If you want a list of that vendor's specific breakdown, don't be afraid to ask for an itemized list. Speaking in general terms, the service charge covers the venue/caterer's labor and administrative costs. An "event production fee" or "the cost of doing business" are other ways to think of it.

30

Do I need to tip on top?

Gratuity to the staff isn't something you are obligated to do; however, I will say that it is pretty customary. Double check your catering contract, as some caterers include this in their initial estimate. Others will leave a line on the final invoice where you can write in the gratuity either before or after the event and run it through with the final payment.

Finding Wedding Professionals Best for You

Top tips for hiring your photographer

First, research and determine what style you like, such as formal, candid or photojournalist. Review your venue's preferred list, and look at portfolios of photographers you are drawn to. Before meeting with them, figure out how long you would like them for and let them know if you are doing an elaborate getaway or not seeing each other before. Ask their opinion. But most of all you must like them. They are with you ALL DAY!

Reminders for choosing your wedding DJ

When meeting with potential DJs, think about how many hours you want them. Do you want sound during the ceremony? Even if you have a string quartet, they will need to be heard, so two sound systems are needed, one for the ceremony and one for the reception. When should they arrive to set up, and should they announce the formalities? Find a time to meet to go over the day and music choices.

33

Maybe you will want a band.

When considering a band, think about how many members there are, and how many hours they will be there, because there will be additional meals to order for them. How much space do they need? When will they arrive to set up, and can they set up before the ceremony? Will someone announce the formalities? How many breaks will they take and do they have suggestions on how to have music during that time?

Darling, you look fabulous: bridal gown

Look through magazines or Pinterest and mark your favorite dresses as well as those with specific things you like about them. Also think about where you are getting married and whether the dress fits the venue. Have the dress photos with you at the venue appointments. Remember to make appointments with bridal shops to ensure someone is set aside just for you. Bring someone with you to take notes and photos.

Paper: the mood and style impression

Paper products give the the first impression of your wedding, and should set the mood and style. Send Save the Dates out six months in advance. Invitations are sent six to eight weeks prior to the wedding. You do not need to order for each guest, but for households. As a rule of thumb, order 75 percent of your guest count. RSVPs should come back to you three to four weeks prior to the wedding. Remember to PROOF everything.

Let them eat cake or desserts

First question: Do you like cake? If not, that is OK, you don't have to serve cake! I have planned plenty of weddings with all types of desserts. When setting up your meetings with dessert vendors, ask when their tastings are, and whether they are done individually or in groups. Also ask if there is a fee for the tasting, and if that fee is credited to you if you hire them.

Looking fabulous with hair and makeup

When you start thinking about this topic, decide if you want your bridal party to have their hair and/or makeup done. If you don't want to pay for it but still want them to be done, talk with your bridal party first. Do a trial run. When setting up timing, work with your photographer on when they need you to be ready, then work backwards to find when you need to start.

38

Darling, you look fabulous: bridesmaid dresses

Have a girl's day. Go out for brunch and then head to a bridal salon and just look at bridesmaid dresses. Talk about what they want and what you want and see if there is a happy medium. Do you want the same color, but they can choose the style, do you want all the same dress and color? Or something in between?

Darling, you look fabulous: groom suit

Go with your groom to help him pick out the suit or tux for him and the groomsmen. If your groomsmen and fathers are across the nation, then using *Men's Wearhouse* is great. You start the order, and the guys can each go to their local store and get measured. Suits can be picked up and dropped off somewhere closer to the venue. HAVE THEM TRY ON THE SUITS when they pick them up.

Let's ride: transportation for wedding day

What do you need? A shuttle to take the wedding party from the getting-ready spot to the venue? Something between the church and the reception? A getaway car at the end of the night? Work on timing first, which will help the company give you a more accurate estimate. If they offer split hours, you can split between the morning/afternoon shuttle and the getaway car.

Design Tips to Rock Your Space

41

There is nothing wrong with rentals.

Depending on your venue, you may have to rent tables and chairs. If you are looking to purchase items for your wedding, consider renting first. It may be a bit more in cost, but you won't have to store items before and after the wedding or find someone to purchase them after the wedding. Renting linens is a great way to bring in color without a lot of cost.

# Shining the light on wedding lighting

Lighting can make a big impact for a very low cost. If you do not have a lot to spend on décor, lighting is amazing in what it can do to a room. The impact is much greater than centerpieces. Most DJs offer lighting packages, but it can also be supplied by event lighting companies, which sometimes have more options. Lighting can accent walls, columns, or any architectural features in the venue.

Floral and décor tips for you

If there is a wall with an unsightly sink or artwork, drape the wall. If the venue is everything you ever wanted except for one thing on one or two walls, draping can help. Find out from your venue when the florist/designer can come to set up. Have them drop off personal flowers to where you are getting ready, then go to the venue for setup.

Venue and styling-- matching your vision

When looking at venues, make sure the one you choose matches your style. I worked with a couple who looked at more than forty venues. The bride had a style she wanted and would not stop until they found it. When they did and the wedding day arrived, the reception was EXACTLY what she wanted. So, really take the time to figure out your style and what you will and will not compromise.

How to stretch your décor budget

Floral and décor is usually twenty percent of your budget. If this is in your top three "wants," then go ahead and add a few more percentage points to the number. To help reduce the cost, use more in-season floral and re-use ceremony floral at the reception (see lesson 48). Reducing the number of boutonnieres and bouquets and corsages for family members also cuts costs.

The difference between florists and designers

A florist and a designer can be the same person, but not all florists are designers. When you meet with your florist, ask if they can help with the entire look of your wedding, from day-of paper products to floral. If they can't, then that is where a designer can step in and create the entire look of your wedding. Some designers even offer to help you with attire.

To DIY or not to DIY

If you love to DIY, that's great, because a wedding is a wonderful opportunity to do some projects. Set a deadline for when these projects are to be done, and if they are not, have a backup plan for replacements or passing the project to a professional. Doing your own flowers is not recommended, but invites, signage and favors are great for DIY!

Ways to repurpose your ceremony floral

When planning décor for the ceremony, make sure that it can be re-used for the reception. If they are at two different places, make sure the floral placement is approved by the church and the florist will move them from one location to the other. The aisle arrangements can be used for the centerpieces at dinner. An altar piece can be used for the head table.

Making it personal-- who needs floral?

When working on your budget, make sure you have enough for bouquets and boutonnieres for the wedding party and parents. This is the minimum you would need. The last thing you want to worry about is having to make them the night before your wedding. Some traditions call for more corsages and boutonnieres, so before meeting with the florist have a list of how many you need of bouquets, boutonnieres, and corsages.

50

Maximize your ceremony floral for reception.

Think about how many tables you have for guests to be seated at. I usually start off with ten people per table, so if you are having one hundred people for the dinner reception, you will need ten centerpieces. Follow the tips in the previous lessons for re-using your ceremony pieces, then see if you can use all aisle pieces or if you need to add a few extra.

Ceremony: More than just "I Do"

Getting to the church on time

If you are getting married inside a church, then meet with the priest, rabbi, minister, elder, or wedding coordinator to find out about church guidelines. Do you need to go to pre-marital counseling or classes? Are there restrictions on using the church or altar areas? Who will be your contact throughout the planning process? Are there restrictions on where the photographer can be? Finally, when can you have a rehearsal?

52

How to find the perfect officiant

If you are getting married outside of the church, then decide if the two of you would like to have a non-denominational officiant perform the ceremony. Does the officiant have a workbook to guide you through writing your vows and customizing the ceremony? How many times do you meet throughout the planning process? Will he or she be there for the rehearsal? When will he or she arrive on the wedding day?

Ceremony music: the dos and don'ts

If you are getting married at a church, then consider string players, a guitarist or a harpist. If you are at a wedding venue, decide if you would like to have a DJ or strings. Strings are nice, but a DJ can be more budget-friendly. Talk to the DJ about what they can play for the ceremony that is appropriate.

54

What is etiquette for ceremony seating?

From the back of the aisle, the bride side is the left side, and the groom side is the right. I had one couple change it up on me and it was fine. Leave the first row on either side for family. The first seat on either side is for the mothers, or a special woman in your life. If parents are divorced, I usually suggest the father sit in the next row.

Wedding party processional: down the aisle

The standard processional consists of the officiant, grandparents, groom's parents with groom, bride's mother, bridesmaids with or without groomsmen, flower girl(s) and ring bearer(s), bride and father. While this is the usual, you can have the groom and the groomsmen come in together, or have the groom come in with the officiant. If there is an uneven number of bridesmaids to groomsmen I suggest the groomsmen come in with the groom.

Wedding recessional: back up the aisle

After the kiss, the couple goes up the aisle first, then bridesmaids and groomsmen come to the center of the aisle and walk up, and so on until the entire wedding party has gone back up the aisle. Then the first row of the groom's side goes, then the first row of the bride's side goes. The officiant then leaves. Ushers or groomsmen come down the aisle and release the rows of the remaining guests.

What does a ceremony look like?

The suggested ceremony outline is: Welcome, Blessing, Reading, Introduction to Vows, Exchange of Vows, Blessing over Rings, Exchange of Rings, Closing, Declaration, Presentation and Kiss. If you want to add a unity candle or any other unity ceremony, do it, but add music while lighting the candles, as it gets really quiet if you don't! Work with your officiant to make it your own.

58

Tips on having friends/family officiate

If you decide to have a friend or family member perform your ceremony, here is the link to become ordained: ULC.org. Order the book, *The Distinctive Wedding Ceremony* by Mary Calhoun to help them be the best officiant for you. They should be at the rehearsal to go over timing and work through the processional and recessional a few times. They are also in charge of the marriage license.

What is in a wedding program?

The program gives your guests something to read while waiting for the ceremony to start. It tells who is in the wedding party and how the ceremony will be performed. It can also thank the guests for coming and honor loved ones who have passed. With that being said, it is also one of the first things I cut when the budget is going over, because most them get recycled.

60

How to get your marriage license

Check your county, but usually you have sixty days before your wedding, but no later than three business days before your wedding to get your license form. One sheet is the official paper that needs to be mailed back after the wedding, which records your marriage. Fill it out before the wedding but sign it at the wedding. The other is a "pretty" certificate that can be filled out later.

Wedding Party: What Do They Do?

61

Who to choose? bridesmaids and groomsmen

Choose wisely who will help with chores during the wedding week and help with the bridal shower. Make sure they won't be sour or bitter about it being all about you at the end of the day. You should both think carefully about who you want in the wedding party. It does not need to be an even number of people on each side.

It is not cheap: who pays?

It is not cheap to be in a wedding party. If paying for the bridal parties' hair and makeup, dress, etc. is not part of your budget then let them know. Be upfront about their estimated costs. I have seen plenty of bridesmaids back out because they could not afford everything associated with the cost of being in the wedding party.

Who to invite to all parties?

Invite only those who you are inviting to the wedding to any other parties or showers. This means the wedding party, family members you are inviting to the wedding, and friends who are coming to the wedding. DO NOT invite a family member or close friend a mom is pushing for if they are not coming to the wedding. Guests expect that if you invited them to one party, they will be a guest at your wedding.

Engagement party: what is the deal?

According to etiquette, this is usually hosted by the parents of the bride, but nowadays it is also a great way to get all the friends and family together and announce your engagement. You can do this at your home or a restaurant. It is not as formal as it was back in the day. Most couples I know just have their close friends over and have a dinner party.

What to register for and where

Amazon, Target, REI, Home Depot . . . . Long gone are the days when you just went to your local department store and registered for china. Now you can register for pretty much anything. This is the time to upgrade dishes, small appliances, sheets, towels, etc., if you are living together already. If you are not living together, take stock of what is coming from each house and start making a list of what you need.

More wedding registry tips and tricks

Register before the bridal shower and make sure you are updating frequently. A rule of thumb is to register for the number of people invited to the wedding, so if you have one hundred people coming to the wedding, register for one hundred gifts. Then add the number of people invited to the bridal shower. If you have multiple showers, make sure you have enough options for them to purchase.

Let's party: bachelorette and bachelor parties

Do not do this the day before the wedding, in fact I wouldn't do it the week of either. A month before is great, which gives everyone enough time to recover. Talk with your wedding party about what you would like to have happen and not happen. Communication is the key for these events. Let the organizer know if there are any budget restrictions for others in the wedding party.

68

The last dinner: rehearsal/welcome dinner

The rehearsal dinner can also be called a welcome dinner, depending on whether or not you are having a destination wedding. Traditionally, this is for the wedding party, immediate family and grandparents. If you have a contingent of family from out of town it is nice to invite them, but it is not necessary. It is usually hosted by the groom's family and it's more of a roast than toast type event.

The next day: post wedding brunch

Back in the day, all the families got together the day after the wedding to watch the couple open their gifts. While this is not the case nowadays, the brunch is. You can make it an afternoon barbecue or whatever you want; it is just a great way to bring family and close friends together. Open your gifts in private if you like--don't bore your guests, just enjoy their company.

Now it's time to open gifts.

For gifts received before the wedding, open and write a thank-you card right away. For those cards and gifts brought to the wedding, my suggestion is to open them before your leave on your honeymoon, writing down who gave you what. Etiquette says you have six months to write thank-you cards, but do it sooner--it will make all parties feel better!

Making the Most of Wedding Week

71

Who's coming for dinner? guest count

If your guest count goes down or up, make sure you tell your venue, caterer and florist, the earlier the better. This will affect the number of tables, chairs, food and centerpieces they will prepare for your wedding. The food count is usually due a few weeks before the wedding. If the guest count becomes higher than what you gave them, let them know as early as possible.

72

Please do feed the wedding pro.

The month of your wedding you should be having finalization meetings with all of your vendors, and making sure you are up to date with payments. For your planner, photographer and DJ, talk to them about their needs for a meal and if they have an assistant with them. Then let your venue/caterer know the vendor meal count.

Seating chart: where to seat guests

This task sneaks up on everyone! To stay ahead of the curve, have a plan in place after you send out the invites. Then create a diagram with the tables needed and as RSVPs come in, place sticky notes or flags with names at specific tables on your diagram. Then each week, review the diagram and move the sticky notes as needed until you have the final product.

Signage: telling guests where to go

It depends on your wedding, but the standard is that you will need escort cards (table where they are sitting) and if you want them at a specific chair, you need a place card at their seat. Programs, menus, signage for guest book and gift table are all options. Decide what you need and work with your printer to have everything ready in time for your wedding.

Making it official: signing marriage license

I always suggest to my couples to sign it after photos are finished and before the ceremony. I have the photographer find a cool spot at the venue if they are seeing each other before the wedding. If you are not seeing each other before, work with the officiant and photographer on where to meet right after the wedding with everyone who is signing the marriage certificate.

Tipping etiquette: who do you tip?

For a helpful blog post on tipping, go to TaylordEvents.com/blog and search for tipping. Expect to tip your transportation and hair and makeup pros ten to twenty percent of their total service. If you are using valet parking, then it is 50 cents to $2 per car. Optional wedding professionals to tip would be: DJ-$50 to $100, musicians-$10 to $100 per musician, photographer, videographer or planner– ten to twenty percent.

Tipping etiquette: wedding day best practices

Put the tips in sealed and labeled envelopes a few days before the wedding. If you are working with a planner, give them the envelopes at the rehearsal and they will hand them out on the day of the wedding, or if you do not have a planner, ask the Best Man or Maid of Honor to pass them out on the day of the wedding.

Gifts for parents and wedding party

Depending on the wedding party, if you are not paying for their hair and makeup or dress, consider giving them something to wear with the dress, such as earrings, bracelets or necklaces. For the guys, it can be cufflinks or something that fits their personalities. For parents, think about activities they like to do, or a frame for your upcoming wedding photo.

911: we have an emergency kit.

If you have a planner, they will be bringing a kit. If you just need the basics, here you go: phone chargers, breath mints or gum, blotting papers, tweezers, clear nail polish, tissues, hairspray, stain remover, fashion tape, aspirin, bandages, glue, wine stain remover, water and protein bars. Make sure you have the lipstick and powder your makeup artist used for touchups.

80

Tips and tricks for the dress

The week leading up to the wedding, make sure your dress is steamed and ready to go. You might want to take it out of the bag and let it air out in a sterile room. Make sure someone knows how to help you bustle the dress. On the day of the wedding, most planners will not take the dress, so take it with you to where you are getting ready.

Let it Go: Wedding Day Bliss

Photos: let your photographer help you

Work with your photographer to create a realistic photo list for the number of hours they will be on-site and if you are seeing each other beforehand. My suggestion is to see each other before. It makes the day easier for all involved and could help your budget by allowing a shorter cocktail hour. If you are not doing a first look, then make sure you have a longer cocktail hour to have enough time for all of your wedding party and couple photos.

Getting ready on the wedding day

Make sure you know where you are getting ready at least a month beforehand, then let the bridal party, hair and makeup artist and photographer know. If it is at the venue, check to see if you can bring in outside food and beverage. Make sure everyone eats and has plenty of water. For the guys, have them arrive an hour before the photos to get ready.

Wedding party duties the day of

This is the time for the wedding party to do their jobs. They will help get the couple ready and where they need to be on time. They help the photographer if needed throughout the day. They make sure the couple eats throughout the day, and that they have their meals and beverages of choice during the reception. They put presents in the car and pack up the couple's stuff for the honeymoon suite.

How to keep the parents sane

There is a lot of emotion for the couple on the day of the wedding, but also for the parents. Be prepared with a handkerchief or tissue for them. You may want to assign a bridesmaid and groomsman to help with the parents. Make sure you have discussed roles throughout the planning process. Let them know you love them and you want them to enjoy the day as well.

Who toasts and when to toast

Who is on the list of toasting? Maid of Honor, Best Man, Bride's Dad and couple. If you want to add more you can, but this is the standard I use. If you are not working with a planner, have the Maid of Honor and the Best Man work with the DJ or band on timing. I suggest toasting with what is in hand, which means guests toast with whatever they are drinking.

Formal dances: the details and tips

First Dance, Father/Daughter Dance and Mother/Son Dance are the formal dances. You can do all three, or you can do none, it is totally up to you, but I do suggest keeping the First Dance. If you don't want to be the center of attention, work with your DJ or band to only play a portion of the song, then you are only dancing for a minute or two instead of three or four minutes.

How to make a great timeline

When working on the timeline, I start with the ceremony time and work my way to the end of the night. I allot thirty minutes for ceremony and forty-five to sixty minutes for cocktail hour. Work with your caterer on how long it will take for dinner, but usually an hour to ninety minutes works. Keep in mind when you need to be out of the venue. The middle of the timeline is for toasts, cake cutting and formal dances.

88

Continuing the making of a timeline

After I finish the reception timeline, I then work from the ceremony back to when the bride needs to start, working my way toward when the bride needs to be ready. This is when you need to communicate with your photographer and hair and makeup artist. The number of photographer hours will dictate when they need to arrive for the shots of you getting into your dress and the last touchup of makeup.

89

What to do with the gifts

Are you at a hotel or a venue? If you are staying at the same hotel for the night, have your Maid of Honor work with the staff on getting everything into your room. If you are at a venue, figure out where you want the gifts to end up. I suggest having them go with a parent. Have someone from the wedding party load up the car. It's a good idea to have this done right after the formalities.

90

Guests are there to see you!

They really want to spend time with you so I suggest you do a first look, which gives you more time with your guests. Take the time to walk around to each table and thank them for coming. They will do what you are doing, so if you want a dance party, then get out there and dance. If you are socializing, so will they.

How to Beat the Wedding Blues

How to keep ahead of thank-you's

If you get a present sent to the house before the wedding, write a thank-you note immediately. It keeps you on top of the task and not stressed after the wedding by writing cards. You may not send them until after the wedding, but get them ready to go and all you'll have to do is write them for those who brought gifts and cards to the wedding, then mail them all out.

Questions: getting the dress clean afterwards

Most dry cleaners now have the option to clean wedding dresses. Ask your regular dry cleaner their process and whether they send wedding dresses out, and if so, where. Do they preserve or just clean? How long can it be boxed up? How long does it take to get back? Can they do the veil as well?

How to get the official certificate

Most of the time, the marriage license has been registered one to two weeks after the wedding. Check with your county regarding their process time and cost of getting certified copies, which you'll need if you are changing your name. Once this is done, then pick them up or have them mail certified copies to you.

94

First steps on changing your name

If you are changing your name, start reviewing what you need to do before the wedding. Make a list of credit cards, utilities, rent, mortgage, passport, social security number, driver license, and anything else you want to change. This will help you figure out how many certified copies of the marriage certificate you need. Then start planning out when you can get it done after the wedding.

95

Loved your vendors? Give them testimonials.

Your wedding professionals get most of their gigs by word of mouth and reviews. Take the time to review them via Facebook, Yelp, and/or Wedding Wire. Be fair when giving a review, and give information that would be helpful to other couples. If something went wrong, bring it up to the professional first, especially if they did not know about it. There's nothing worse than being blindsided by a bad review.

What to do with the stuff

What did you purchase for the wedding that you no longer need? Search to see if there are Facebook groups in your area for other couples to sell to each other. If you are in the Seattle area, go to *GetHitchedGiveHope.com* to see how you can donate to HopeChest, a wedding rummage sale that gives all proceeds to the Dream Foundation and the Young Survival Foundation.

97

Photos are ready! Order your album.

Roughly six weeks after the wedding, depending on your photographer, you get to relive the wedding all over again with the photos! Spend time with your partner to review photos and pick sixty to one hundred photos for the album and then meet with your photographer get their favorites so you can get the album created and ordered. While you are at it, order albums for parents, they make great gifts.

98

Now to return/exchange and purchase.

Review the gifts and look for duplicates, things not on the registry you want to exchange, and items that need to be purchased. Take time to go over everything you have, including what is currently being used that can be donated and replaced. This is the time to do it! Just make sure you let the people who gave you gift cards know what you purchased on their behalf.

… 99

How to get over the letdown

Reconnect with friends and family, since planning can take time away from them. Reinstate date nights and girlfriend days. Get back to what you did before wedding planning consumed your every waking moment. Work out, read, or find a new hobby, maybe something you and your partner can do together. Maybe start planning that next big trip! My husband and I started road-tripping around the state.

100

Open the bubbly. Enjoy married life!

That is it! There's not much else to say for this lesson, except congratulations and enjoy married life!

About the *Six-Word Lessons Series*

Legend has it that Ernest Hemingway was challenged to write a story using only six words. He responded with the story, "For sale: baby shoes, never worn." The story tickles the imagination. Why were the shoes never worn? The answers are left up to the reader's imagination.

This style of writing has a number of aliases: postcard fiction, flash fiction, and micro fiction. Lonnie Pacelli was introduced to this concept in 2009 by a friend, and started thinking about how this extreme brevity could apply to today's communication culture of text messages, tweets and Facebook posts. He wrote the first book, *Six-Word Lessons for Project Managers*, then started helping other authors write and publish their own books in the series.

The books all have six-word chapters with six-word lesson titles, each followed by a one-page description. They can be written by entrepreneurs who want to promote their businesses, or anyone with a message to share.

See the entire *Six-Word Lessons Series* at **6wordlessons.com**

www.ingramcontent.com/pod-product-compliance
Lightning Source LLC
LaVergne TN
LVHW051645080426
835511LV00016B/2503